KILLING YAMAMOTO

KILLING YAMAMOTO

*The American Raid
That Avenged Pearl Harbor*

DANIEL HAULMAN

NEWSOUTH BOOKS

Montgomery

NewSouth Books
105 S. Court Street
Montgomery, AL 36104

Publisher's Cataloging-in-Publication data

Haulman, Daniel
Killing Yamamoto : the American raid that avenged Pearl Harbor / Daniel Haulman
p. cm.

ISBN 978-1-60306-387-6 (paperback)
ISBN 978-1-60306-388-3 (ebook)

1. Yamamoto, Isoroku, 1884–1943—Assassination. 2. World War, 1939–1945—
Campaigns—Pacific Area. 3. World War, 1939–1945—Aerial operations, American.
I. Title.

2015930564

Printed in the United States of America

To my twin brother,
Colonel David Haulman,
a retired Air Force pilot

CONTENTS

Isoroku Yamamoto

I. The Background of the Mission

Of all the enemies of the United States during World War II, one of the most hated was Admiral Isoroku Yamamoto, commander of the Combined Japanese Imperial Fleet. He had planned the sneak attack on Pearl Harbor that had killed more than 2,400 Americans on December 7, 1941. He had also planned the attack on Midway in mid-1942, which, although a decisive American victory, resulted in many American casualties. One of the primary reasons why the United States won the Battle of Midway was because American intelligence had broken the Japanese code. If American planners had not discovered the Japanese plans in advance, Yamamoto might have succeeded in the eventual conquest of the Hawaiian Islands.

The same kind of American intelligence revealed that in April 1943 Yamamoto was scheduled to make an inspection flight from Rabaul to Ballale, near Bougainville, in the northern Solomon Islands. He had never before come so close to American lines. The message contained details about exactly where he would be and when. US Marine Corps Major Alva Bryan "Red" Lasswell, an intelligence analyst at Pearl Harbor's Fleet Radio Unit, Pacific, among others, received and decoded the key message. The information revealed that Admiral Yamamoto would be flying aboard a Mitsubishi G4M medium twin-engine bomber the Allies called a "Betty," and it would be escorted by six Zero fighters. The Betty bomber had a reputation for long-range flight because of its large fuel capacity, but for that same reason it was especially vulnerable to enemy aircraft fire. Yamamoto also had a reputation for punctuality—if he planned to be at a certain place at a certain time, he would be there.

When Admiral Chester W. Nimitz, commander of the U.S. Pacific Fleet, learned of this intelligence, he notified authorities in Washington, who endorsed a bold mission to assassinate the Japanese admiral. Nimitz contacted Admiral William F. Halsey, commander in the South Pacific, who assigned the project to Rear Admiral Marc A. Mitscher, commander of joint air operations in the Solomons. The assignment was appropriate. Mitscher had been commander of the U.S.S. *Hornet*, the aircraft carrier from which

Jimmy Doolittle had launched the first raid on Japan on April 18, 1942, exactly a year before the anticipated Yamamoto flight.

II. THE PLANNING

Planners of the mission to assassinate Yamamoto gathered on Guadalcanal, the American-held island closest to Bougainville. Several officers took part in the initial planning. Besides Mischner, they included his chief of staff Gen. Field Harris, Commander Stanhope C. Ring, and Col. Edwin L. Pugh, and Maj. John P. Condon of Fighter Command, Solomons. They were all naval or Marine Corps personnel. Lt. Col. Aaron W. Tyer, commander of one of the Army Air Forces airfields on Guadalcanal, and commander of the 18th Fighter Group, also contributed ideas related to his resources. The planners decided the raiders would have to counter Japanese radar by flying low, avoiding a direct route over Japanese-held islands between Guadalcanal and Bougainville, and keeping radio silence. The circuitous route between Guadalcanal and Bougainville and back would require fighters that could fly more than 400 miles to the target and then return. The only fighter planes on Guadalcanal with such a range were Army Air Forces P-38s with special drop tanks. Consequently, the mission was assigned to Army Air Forces organizations already based on the island. They included the 12th and 70th Fighter Squadrons of the 18th Fighter Group and the 339th Fighter Squadron of the 347th Fighter Group. Pilots of those squadrons were selected to take part in the mission, some to attack the Yamamoto airplane, and others to escort them. They served as a special detachment under the Thirteenth Air Force.

Maj. John W. Mitchell commanded the 339th Fighter Squadron, and he assumed command of the mission. In consultation with Lt. Col. Henry Vicellio from Thirteenth Air Force headquarters, Mitchell decided to hit

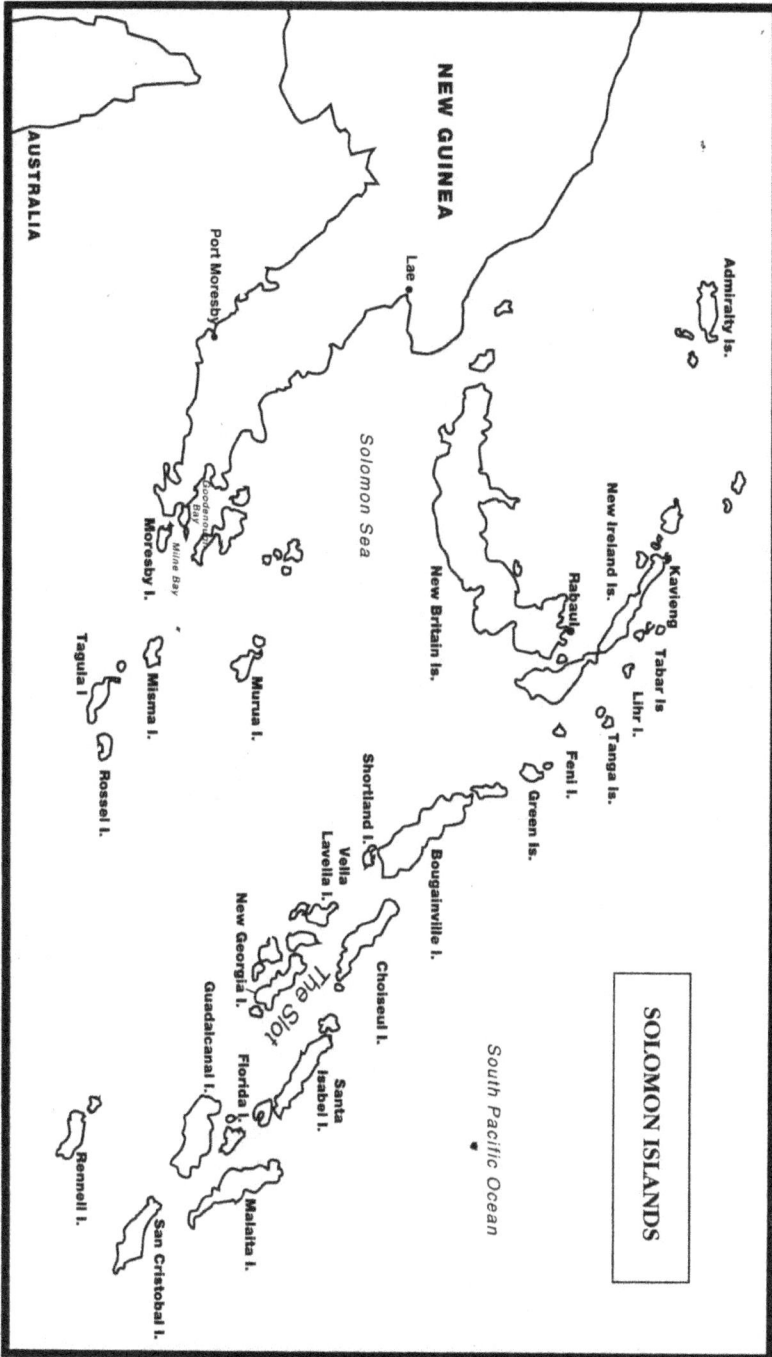

SOLOMON ISLANDS

NEW GUINEA

AUSTRALIA

Port Moresby

Lae

Admiralty Is.

New Ireland Is.

Kavieng

Rabaul

New Britain Is.

Tabar Is

Lihr I.

Tanga Is.

Feni I.

Green Is.

Solomon Sea

Goodenough Bay

Milne Bay

Moresby I.

Tagula I.

Misma I.

Murua I.

Rossel I.

Shortland I.

Vella Lavella I.

New Georgia I.

The Slot

Bougainville I.

Choiseul I.

Santa Isabel I.

Guadalcanal I.

Florida Is.

Malaita I.

Rennell I.

San Cristobal I.

South Pacific Ocean

A P-38 fighter.

Yamamoto while he was still in the air over Bougainville, rather than after he landed, because there was more likelihood he would not survive such an attack. On the evening of April 17, Major Mitchell converted the flight navigation plan he received from Major Condon into detailed instructions for his pilots. He planned for eighteen P-38s to be involved, fourteen (which he would lead himself) to ward off Japanese escort fighters, and four for the attacking flight.

III. THE MISSION BEGINS

Two of the eighteen P-38s had to abort from the mission when it launched on Sunday morning, April 18, the anniversary of the Doolittle raid. One blew a tire on takeoff, and the other failed to draw fuel from its drop tanks. The sixteen remaining P-38s continued on the mission, two reassigned from attack to escort duty.

The long flight from Guadalcanal to Bougainville covered more than 400 miles and took about two hours. The formation went west for 183 miles, then turned northwest for another 88 miles, then turned even more northward for another 125 miles. Sixteen miles from Bougainville, the P-38s turned northeastward on a path expected to take them into the right side of the group of planes in which Yamamoto was riding, since that flight was expected to be flying southeastward.

The Japanese formation in which Yamamoto was flying included eight airplanes, not one but two GM4 "Betty" bombers being used as transports for Yamamoto and his staff, and the expected six Zero escort fighters to protect them. The Japanese airplanes left Rabaul about 8:00 (American time), flying southeastward, and arrived over southern Bougainville (island) about 9:34, for about 1 hour, 34 minutes flying time. The Japanese formation flew at an altitude of 6,500 feet most of the way, but descended over southern Bougainville to a little over 2,000 feet, preparing to land either at an airfield on the southern end of the island or at Ballale, small island just

A Mitsubishi GM4 "Betty" bomber.

south of Bougainville.

The American formation led by Col. John Mitchell included sixteen P-38 fighters, four in the attack flight and twelve as escorts. The four in the attack flight were led by Captain Thomas G. Lanphier Jr. The other pilots included Lieutenant Rex T. Barber, Lanphier's wingman, and Lieutenant Besby F. Holmes and his wingman Raymond K. Hine. All sixteen pilots left Guadalcanal about 7:25 American time and arrived at Bougainville about 9:34, for a flying time of about 2 hours and 9 minutes to the target. Although they flew generally northwest, the route was circuitous. Total flying time, to target and back, was more than four hours. The American P-38s flew at an altitude of less than 1,000 feet most of the way, over the water, to avoid detection. They climbed in the vicinity of Bougainville, the attack flight to the level of the expected Japanese bombers, and the escorts to a much higher altitude to counter any Japanese fighter opposition from other airfields in the vicinity. Most P-38s could fly at a maximum speed of more than 400 miles per hour, but the P-38s on this mission flew more like 200 miles per hour, because they carried an extraordinary heavy load of fuel in special larger auxiliary tanks designed for the mission, two per plane (which they dropped upon reaching the target area). Also slowing the P-38s was the low altitude of most of the flight, where the air was denser.

IV. The Attack

As the P-38s approached Bougainville, they encountered the airplanes in the Yamamoto flight at the expected place and time. The meticulous planning, along with Yamamoto's reputation for punctuality, benefitted the raiders. Major Mitchell led twelve of the P-38s on a climb to at least 15,000 feet to meet the swarm of Japanese Zero fighters he expected to emerge from Kahili, a Japanese airfield on Bougainville, and to confront the six Zeros

A Mitsubishi A6M "Zero" fighter.

escorting the Yamamoto bomber. The other four P-38s, flown by Lanphier, Barber, Holmes, and Hine, went after Yamamoto.

The surprise for the American P-38 pilots was that there were two Japanese Betty bombers, the type American intelligence had indicated would be carrying Yamamoto. The Americans did not know which held their prey. They dropped their auxiliary fuel tanks, now almost empty, in order to gain increased speed and maneuverability.

Something went wrong. When Holmes tried to drop his fuel tanks, they would not fall. He turned violently away, hoping the acceleration would allow him to get rid of the tanks for combat, and when he did, his wingman Hine followed him. That took half of the four-plane attacking flight away from the scene, temporarily, leaving only the two flown by Lanphier and Barber to face the two Japanese bombers and their six escorting fighters. For a short time over Bougainville, it was two against eight. The odds did not look good. The other P-38s were high above, looking for enemy fighters to emerge from Bougainville's airfields.

Lanphier turned into the Zero escorts, while Barber went after one of the bombers, which was diving rapidly to avoid him. Barber chased and fired, hitting the Betty from behind. Barber then temporarily lost sight of his prey, but when he turned to look back, he could see a bomber crash into the jungle, and assumed he had hit the airplane. He did not know yet whether Yamamoto was aboard that bomber or the other one.

In the meantime, Lanphier, after having taken shots at the Zeros escorting the bombers, flipped over to try to reach one of the bombers. He claimed to have spotted one descending over the island, and fired at it briefly from its right side. Like Barber, Lanphier also saw a Japanese bomber crash into the jungle, with black smoke rising above the palm trees. Like Barber, he thought he had shot down one of the bombers over Bougainville, but did not know whether it was the one carrying Admiral Yamamoto.

Meanwhile, Holmes had managed to get rid of his auxiliary fuel tanks, and he and wingman Hine went after the second bomber. It veered out over the sea south of Bougainville and they shot at it. Barber, having disposed of one bomber over the island, joined Holmes and Hine in attacking the second bomber, and it crashed into the sea. The mission had succeeded. Both bombers had been shot down. Yet no one knew which of the bombers carried Yamamoto, or whether he survived the crash, either on the island or into the sea.

The four pilots in the attack flight immediately headed back toward Guadalcanal, but only three returned safely. Hine disappeared on the mission, probably shot down by one of the six escorting Zeroes, or by other Zeroes from Kahili. The twelve escorting P-38s, their mission accomplished, also returned to Guadalcanal, this time flying on a more direct path.

V. THE DEBRIEFING

When Lanphier, Barber, and Holmes returned to Guadalcanal, they gave intelligence officers an account of what they had experienced. Lanphier claimed to have shot down Yamamoto because he assumed Yamamoto was on the bomber he shot at over Bougainville. Barber also claimed to have shot down Yamamoto, because he assumed that Yamamoto was on the bomber he had shot down over Bougainville. The intelligence officers took their word for having each shot down a bomber over the island, and at first gave them each a credit for having shot down a Japanese bomber over Bougainville. But still, if Yamamoto was on one of two bombers that went down over the island, no one know which one had contained Yamamoto. The other bomber that Holmes and Barber had shot down over the sea was considered at first by intelligence officers to have been a third Betty bomber which had entered the vicinity from elsewhere. The confused officers gave Lanphier and Barber each credit for one bomber over the island, and Holmes and Barber each a half credit for a third bomber over the sea. Hine, the P-38 pilot who had failed to return, got no credit.

What had actually happened? There were only two Betty bombers in the Yamamoto flight. The one that was shot down over the island of Bougainville did indeed contain Admiral Yamamoto. Part of the admiral's staff was on the other bomber that went down at sea, and some of those passengers survived.

Although the American pilots thought they had shot down Yamamoto, they could not announce that publicly. If the Japanese learned that the Americans knew they had gotten Yamamoto immediately after he was lost, they would have known that their codes had been broken. Despite Lanphier's eagerness to claim he had shot down Yamamoto, he and the other pilots were told to keep their mouths shut about the still-classified operation.

The Japanese themselves were not eager to announce that Admiral Yamamoto had been shot down over Bougainville on April 18, 1943, because that would have lowered morale. They first wanted to make sure he was not among the survivors. But they found his body, easily identifiable because the admiral had lost two fingers in a naval engagement during the Russo-Japanese War. His body was recovered on Bougainville and returned by ship to Japan. When the Japanese finally admitted that their famous admiral had been lost in combat, the Americans could then announce that they had shot him down, although under the pretense it was a lucky shot during aerial combat over the Solomon Islands.

Eventually the Americans realized that there were only two Betty bombers on the Yamamoto flight, and that a third bomber had not entered the scene. Only one bomber had crashed on the island of Bougainville. If Barber and

Lanphier had both shot down a Betty bomber over the island that day, they must have both been shooting at the same airplane. Credit for shooting down Yamamoto's plane, and killing Yamamoto, was split between them, because he had been aboard the airplane that crashed on Bougainville.

Barber at first seemed to have been happy to share half the credit for killing Yamamoto, but Lanphier continued to claim that he alone had achieved that goal. A great controversy brewed for years afterwards over which of the two pilots should have more credit for shooting down Yamamoto. Eventually friends of Barber claimed that Lanphier's account was less credible than Barber's, especially after discovery of the wreckage, and the Japanese autopsy revealed after the war, showed that the Yamamoto airplane went down more as a result of fire from behind than from the right side.

In 1978, the United States Air Force published *USAF Historical Study 85*, which listed the aerial victory credits of the Army Air Forces during World War II. That study awarded half a credit each to Rex T. Barber and Thomas G. Lanphier Jr. for shooting down the bomber carrying Admiral Yamamoto. Because of challenges to that determination, the Air Force called an Air Force victory credit board of review, which met in March 1985 at the Albert F. Simpson Historical Center, now called the Air Force Historical Research Center, at Maxwell Air Force Base. That board, of which the author was a member, determined that the credit was properly split between Lanphier and Barber. Challenges continued, and in 1991, the case was reopened with the Air Force Board for the Correction of Military Records in Washington, D.C. That board used the same evidence, but did not come unanimously, as the first board had, to the same conclusion. It was deadlocked between those who wanted to keep the credit split, and those who wanted to give sole credit to Rex T. Barber. The Secretary of the Air Force at the time, Donald B. Rice, broke the deadlock and decided to keep the credit split. Barber supporters challenged Rice's authority to make that decision, and in March 1996 the Ninth Circuit U.S. Court of Appeals determined that Rice had acted properly. The credit for shooting down Yamamoto remains officially split between Barber and Lanphier.

Recent articles published online and elsewhere sometimes claim that in 2003, the Air Force decided to award full credit for shooting down

Yamamoto's airplane to Rex Barber, and take away the half credit for that plane that belonged to Lanphier. Those articles are wrong. Official aerial victory credits are awarded by the United States Air Force and kept on file at the Air Force Historical Research Agency, where I have worked for more than 32 years. If anyone makes the claim that official credit for the shoot-down of Yamamoto was given to only Barber or only Lanphier, he or she should be able to produce an official USAF document that says so. In this case, they cannot, because such a document does not exist. The new claim is probably based on the 1997 decision by the American Fighter Aces Association to recognize Barber as the only pilot to shoot down Yamamoto's airplane. The American Fighter Aces Association is not part of the United States Air Force, although many if not most of its members are Air Force veterans.

Regardless of who got the aerial victory credit, the mission to kill Yamamoto was a tremendous success. Besides the shooters, the real heroes were mission leader Major John W. Mitchell of the Army Air Forces, mission planner US Marine Corps Major John P. Condon, and code breakers such as Major Alva B. Lasswell, also of the Marine Corps.

VI. RESULTS OF YAMAMOTO'S DEATH

The death of Yamamoto was not just revenge for Pearl Harbor. It deprived the Japanese of one of their greatest strategists and admirals. If Yamamoto had not been killed on April 18, 1943, on the anniversary of the Doolittle Raid, he might have survived to plan more attacks similar to the ones at Pearl Harbor and Midway. Despite the breaking of the Japanese code, those plans might have had some success, resulting in the deaths of many more Americans. As it was, the loss of Yamamoto deprived the Japanese not only of one of their greatest military leaders, but also of a good deal of their morale. At the same time, it eventually bolstered American morale to know that the villain of Pearl Harbor was dead. The Japanese continued to resist American forces advancing in the Pacific, but thereafter those efforts were almost always defensive. In a sense, the shooting down of Admiral Yamamoto can be considered another turning point in World War II.

Some historians suggest that the killing of Admiral Yamamoto was counterproductive. They argue that Yamamoto, despite his belligerence in planning the Pearl Harbor and Midway attacks, was less hard-lined than his Japanese Army counterparts advising the Japanese Emperor, Hirohito, and that his presence might have encouraged Japan to surrender earlier than she did. Others criticize the mission as having been foolhardy, because it might have revealed to the Japanese that their codes had been broken. How else could the Americans have known that Yamamoto was to be flying over Bougainville on April 18, 1943? If the Japanese had changed their codes, American operations in the Pacific might not have been successful. The Japanese did not come to the conclusion that their codes had been broken, and did not change them, possibly because immediately after the mission, American P-38s launched more raids from Guadalcanal to Bougainville. Their primary purpose was to deceive the Japanese into believing that shooting down Yamamoto was just a lucky coincidence.

VII. THE YAMAMOTO 'SHOOT-DOWN' CREDIT CONTROVERSY

- 18 April 1943. A raid by Army Air Force P-38s shot down a G4M "Betty" aircraft carrying Admiral Isoroku Yamamoto, commander of the Japanese Combined Fleet and the planner of both the Pearl Harbor and Midway attacks in 1941 and 1942.
- 11 September 1945. A War Department news release noted that Thomas

Lanphier shot down Admiral Yamamoto's airplane.

- 2 July 1969. A memorandum by Dr. Maurer Maurer, then chief of the Historical Studies Branch of the Aerospace Studies Institute, noted that since both Lanphier and Barber reported having shot down one bomber over Bougainville, and since only one bomber went down over the island, and since Yamamoto was aboard that bomber, credit for the victory should be split, half going to Lanphier and half going to Barber.

- 1978. The Albert F. Simpson Historical Research Center (forerunner of the Air Force Historical Research Agency, in cooperation with Air University and the Office of Air Force History, published USAF Historical Study 85, USAF Credits for the Destruction of Enemy Aircraft, World War II. The study confirmed that Barber and Lanphier each earned half a credit (.5) on April 18, 1943, for having shot down Yamamoto's airplane.

- 1985. Brigadier General Michael Jackson, vice president of the American Fighter Aces Association, pressed the Office of Air Force History to award sole credit for shooting down Yamamoto to Thomas Lanphier.

- March 1985. On the request of Dr. Richard Kohn, head of the Office of Air Force History, the USAF Historical Research Agency (forerunner of the Air Force Historical Research Agency) convened a six-person board of review to reconsider who should have credit for shooting down the Yamamoto airplane. The board decided to keep the credit split, half each for Barber and Lanphier.

- 26 November 1987. Thomas Lanphier died.

- 24 June 1991. Rex Barber applied to the Air Force Board for the Correction of Military Records for a review of the case and requested sole credit for having shot down Yamamoto.

- October 1991. The Air Force Board for the Correction of Military Records held a formal hearing in Washington, DC, to consider the Yamamoto aerial victory credit question. Advocates for Barber, including the Second Yamamoto Mission Association, presented evidence based on a trip to the wreckage site at Bougainville. At the conclusion of the hearing the board could not agree on whether to change the credit from split to full credit for Barber. The hearing findings were presented to

Secretary of the Air Force, Donald B. Rice.

- 11 January 1993. Not long before leaving office as Secretary of the Air Force, Donald Rice decided to keep the credit for shooting down Yamamoto's airplane split between Barber and Lanphier.
- March 1996. The United States Ninth Circuit Court affirmed a lower court decision (United States District Court in Portland) that the Secretary of the Air Force had the authority to make the decision to leave official credit for the Yamamoto shoot-down split evenly between Barber and Lanphier.
- 1997–1998. The American Fighter Aces Association and the Confederate (later Commemorative) Air Force decided to recognize Rex Barber alone as having shot down Yamamoto.
- 26 July 2001. Rex Barber died.

SOURCES OF INFORMATION

Some of the most important primary sources of information regarding the mission to shoot down the Yamamoto aircraft are stored at the Air Force Historical Research Agency, the most important repository of Air Force unit records. Among them are histories of organizations such as the 347th Fighter Group and the 339th Fighter Squadron for the period in question. An example is Kim Daugh's history of the 339th Fighter Squadron for the period 30 Oct 1942-31 Dec 1943, call number SQ-FI-339-HI. Another good primary source is the "Story of the 339th Fighter Squadron," produced by the Thirteenth Air Force Public Relations Office for the period Mar-Apr 1943, call number SQ-FI-339-SU-RE-D at the Air Force Historical Research Agency. There is also a Thirteenth Fighter Command Detachment Combat Report for 18 Apr 1943, also called a debriefing report, at the agency. The agency also maintains an 8 Mar 1989 oral history interview of Cargill Hall with Maj. Gen. John P. Condon, USMC, one of the planners of the mission, with call number K239.0512-1863.

Letters from or to the Yamamoto mission participants relating to the question of whether Thomas Lanphier or Rex Barber should have received sole credit for the shoot-down were some sources for this paper. Among them are a letter from Thomas Lanphier to John Mitchell dated 18 Jul 1984, a letter from Rex Barber to Thomas Lanphier dated 12 Sep 1984, and letter from Thomas Lanphier to Rex Barber dated 18 Sep 1984, a letter from Maj. Gen. John P. Condon to Thomas Lanphier dated 5 Dec 1984, and a letter from Gen. D.C. Strother to Thomas Lanphier dated 21 Jan 1985. Those letters were available to the author and other members of the 1985 Victory Credit Board that considered the case, and furnished information for an article on the Yamamoto mission the author wrote for AIR POWER HISTORY, the periodical publication of the Air Force Historical Foundation, in its summer 2003 issue.

Another good source, from Rex Barber's perspective, is contained in an article called "Rex T. Barber: In His Own Words," contained in the *World War II Jungle Air Force Newsletter* published by the Thirteenth Air Force Veterans as their Fall/Winter 2001 newsletter. For Thomas Lanphier's perspective, there are earlier sources, such as volume 4 of *The Army Air Forces in World War II,* edited by Wesley Frank Craven and James Lea Cate and reprinted by the Office of Air Force History in Washington, DC in 1983. That volume is entitled *The Pacific: Guadalcanal to Saipan, August 1942 to July 1944.* That volume was originally published in 1950, and, like other publications of the time, gave full credit for shooting down Yamamoto's airplane to Thomas Lanphier, who became the first president of the Air Force Association around that time. There is a persistent rumor that Lanphier himself, rather than the usual intelligence officer, typed up the initial report on the mission, which gave him more credit than others thought he deserved.

Among secondary sources, there are some good books on the Yamamoto mission. Burke Davis published *Get Yamamoto* (New York: Random House, 1969), a book that mentions not only what Lanphier but also what Barber and the other pilots in the attack flight accomplished on that fateful day on April 18, 1943. R. Cargill Hall, who once headed the Research Division of the Air Force Historical Research Agency, and in whose office the 1985 victory credit board met, wrote a book called *Lightning Over Bougainville* (Washington, DC: Smithsonian Institution Press, 1991) to defend the conclusion of the board that both Lanphier and Barber shot down the Yamamoto airplane. Two later books on the subject argue that Barber should have full credit, because they discount the Lanphier account of the mission and offer evidence from the discovered wreckage of Yamamoto's airplane. One is *Attack on Yamamoto* (Atglen, PA: Schiffer Military History, 1993) by respected aviation historian Carroll V. Glines. The other is *Lightning Strike* (New York: St. Martin's Griffin, 2005), by Donald A. Davis, which includes more information about the controversy.

Other good secondary sources are books on the breaking of the Japanese code, which made interception of Yamamoto's airplane possible. They include W. J. Holmes, *Double-Edged Secrets: U.S. Naval Intelligence Operations in the Pacific During World War II* (Annapolis, MD: Naval Institute Press, 1979) and Ronald Levin's *The American Magic: Codes, Ciphers and the Defeat of Japan* (New York: Farrar, Straus, Giroux, 1982).

Japanese sources are also valuable in piecing together the Yamamoto mission. One is Hiroyuki Agawa's *The Reluctant Admiral* (Tokyo, Japan: Kodansha International, 1979) and Matome Ugaki, *Fading Victory: The Diary of Admiral Matome Ugaki, 1941-1945* (Pittsburgh, PA: University of Pittsburgh Press, 1991). The first is about Yamamoto, whose bomber went down over the island of Bougainville, and the second is about his chief of staff, whose bomber went down in the sea just south of Bougainville. Both were shot down by the P-38s of Lanphier's four-plane attack flight. Miraculously, Ugaki, whose plane crashed into the water, survived that fateful day on April 18, 1943.

About the Author

Dr. Daniel L. Haulman is Chief, Organization History Division, at the Air Force Historical Research Agency, where he has worked since 1982. He earned his Bachelor's degree from the University of Southwestern Louisiana in 1971, his Master's degree from the University of New Orleans in 1975, and his Ph.D. in history from Auburn University in 1983. His dissertation examined the first state constitutions and how they differed from the colonial frames of government. During the 1970s, he worked at Charity Hospital in New Orleans and taught high school social studies in Louisiana for five years. He has authored seven books about aviation history, including *Air Force Aerial Victory Credits: World War I, World War II, Korea, and Vietnam*; *The United States and Air Force and Humanitarian Airlift Operations, 1947-1994*; *One Hundred Years of Flight: USAF Chronology of Significant Air and Space Events, 1903-2002*; *The Tuskegee Airmen: An Illustrated History, 1939-1949* (with Joseph Caver and Jerome Ennels), *Eleven Myths About the Tuskegee Airmen, The Tuskegee Airmen and the Never Lost a Bomber Myth*, and *What Hollywood Got Right and Wrong About the Tuskegee Airmen*. Dr. Haulman has also written three Air Force pamphlets, including *The High Road to Tokyo Bay; Hitting Home: The Air Offensive Against Japan;* and *Wings of Hope: The U.S. Air Force and Humanitarian Airlift Operations*. He has composed sections of other USAF publications and compiled the list of official USAF aerial victories appearing on the Air Force Historical Research Agency's internet web page. He wrote the Air Force chapter in supplement IV of *A Guide to the Sources of United States Military History* and completed six studies on aspects of recent USAF operations that have been used by the Air Staff and Air University. He has also written two of five chapters in the latest edition of *Locating Air Force Base Sites: History's Legacy*, a book about the location of Air Force bases, and eleven articles in *Short of War*, a book about the United States Air Force in twenty-three contingency operations. The author of more than twenty published articles in various journals, Dr. Haulman has also presented twenty-seven different historical papers at historical conferences and taught ten college courses, one each at Auburn University and Auburn University Montgomery, and four each at Huntingdon College and Faulkner University in Montgomery, Alabama. He is married to Ellen Evans Haulman, and they have a son named Evan.

ALSO BY DANIEL HAULMAN

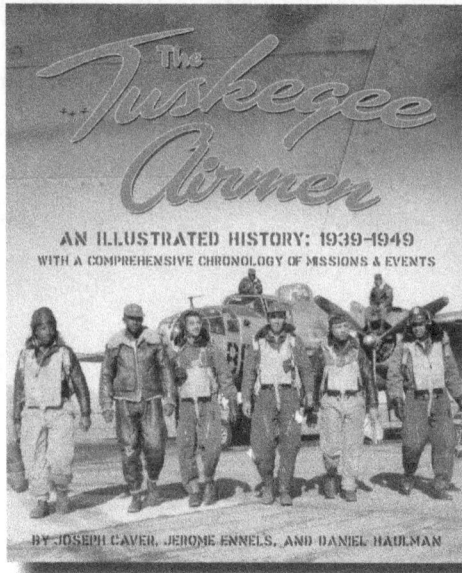

Experience the visual history of the Tuskegee Airmen . . .

Many documentaries, articles, museum exhibits, books, and movies have now treated the subject of the Tuskegee Airmen, the only black American military pilots in World War II. Most of these works have focused on their training and their subsequent accomplishments during combat.

The Tuskegee Airmen: An Illustrated History goes further, using captioned photographs to trace the Airmen through the various stages of training, deployment, and combat in North Africa, Italy, and over occupied Europe. Included for the first time are depictions of the critical support roles of nonflyers: doctors, mechanics, and others, all of whom contributed to the Airmen's success. This volume makes vivid the story of the Tuskegee Airmen and the environments in which they lived, worked, played, fought, and sometimes died.

ISBN 978-1-58838-244-3
Available in hardcover
Visit www.newsouthbooks.com/tuskegeeairmen

ALSO BY DANIEL HAULMAN

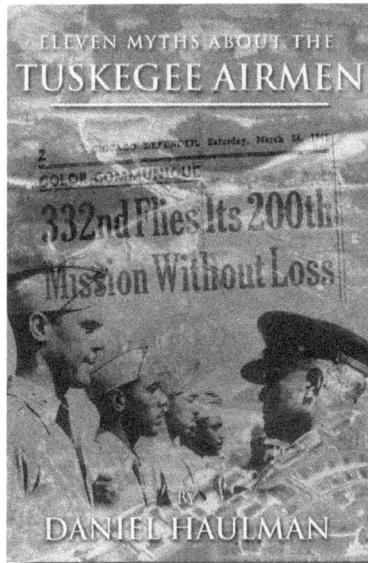

Learn more about the Tuskegee Airmen . . .

The members of the 332d Fighter Group and the 99th, 100th, 301st, and 302d Fighter Squadrons during World War II are remembered in part because they were the only African American pilots who served in combat with the Army Air Forces during the war. They are more often called the Tuskegee Airmen since they trained at Tuskegee Army Air Field. In the more than sixty years since World War II, several stories have grown up about the Tuskegee Airmen, some of them true and some of them false. This book focuses on eleven myths about the Tuskegee Airmen, throughly researched and debunked by Air Force historian Daniel Haulman, with copious historical documentation and sources to prove Haulman's research.

ISBN 978-1-60306-147-6
Available in paperback and ebook
Visit www.newsouthbooks.com/elevenmyths

ALSO BY DANIEL HAULMAN

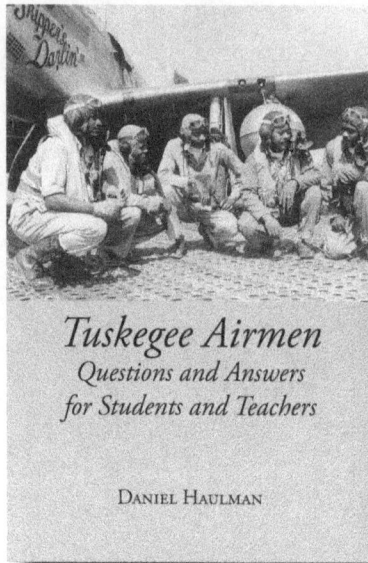

A resource for classrooms or general interest . . .

Almost everyone you meet has heard about the Tuskegee Airmen, but surprisingly few can answer with accuracy questions relating to their most important leaders, aircraft, missions, stations, phases of flight training, and unique accomplishments. Some of the Tuskegee Airmen stories in circulation are downright false. This book, designed primarily for students and teachers but also useful for general readers, answers 76 of the most common questions that people ask about the Tuskegee Airmen, enabling readers to separate the facts from the fictions. This short and accurate summary of Tuskegee Airmen history honors the first African American pilots in U.S. military service—pioneers in the continuing struggle for racial equality.

ISBN 978-1-60306-381-4
Available in paperback and ebook
Visit www.newsouthbooks.com/airmenqa

ALSO BY DANIEL HAULMAN

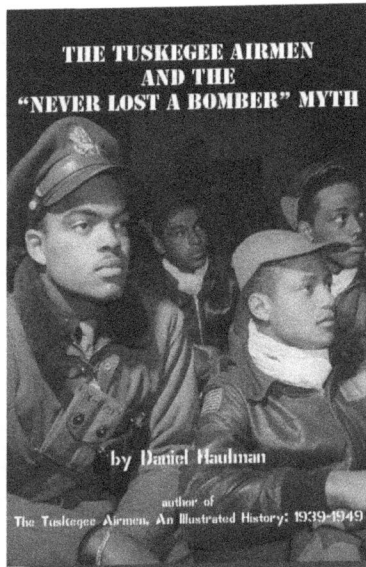

Investigating the "Never Lost a Bomber" myth . . .

During the first sixty years following World War II, a powerful myth grew up claiming that the Tuskegee Airmen, the only black American military pilots in the war, had been the only fighter escort group never to have lost a bomber to enemy aircraft fire. The myth was enshrined in articles, books, museum exhibits, television programs, and films.

This ebook explores how the "never lost a bomber" myth originated and grew, and then refutes it conclusively with careful reference to primary source documents located at the Air Force Historical Research Agency. By piecing together these historical documents, Daniel Haulman not only proves that sometimes bombers under the escort of the Tuskegee Airmen were shot down by enemy aircraft, but when and where those losses occurred, and to which groups they belonged.

ISBN 978-1-60306-105-6
Available as an ebook
Visit www.newsouthbooks.com/bombermyth

ALSO BY DANIEL HAULMAN

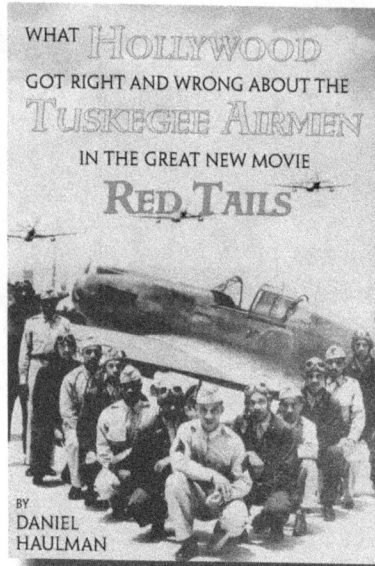

The movie is only the beginning . . .

The new George Lucas movie called *Red Tails* focuses attention on the Tuskegee Airmen of World War II and their combat operations overseas. Loaded with special effects and a great cast, the movie is thrilling and inspiring, but how accurate is it historically? Military historian Daniel Haulman takes an appreciative look at *Red Tails*, comparing it to the actual missions of the Tuskegee Airmen and offering places where interested viewers could study the events further.

"This list of differences between the *Red Tails* depiction of the Tuskegee Airmen and the real Tuskegee Airmen story is not intended to denigrate the movie," Haulman writes in his introduction, "but merely to caution those who might mistakenly take the fictional account as history."

ISBN 978-1-60306-160-5
Available as an ebook
Visit www.newsouthbooks.com/redtails

www.ingramcontent.com/pod-product-compliance
Lightning Source LLC
Chambersburg PA
CBHW021123020426
42331CB00004B/600